THRIVING
IN CHANGING SEASONS

by

'Lanre Somorin M.D.

FAITH2FE
PUBLISHING
Little Rock
2021

Thriving in Changing Seasons

by 'Lanre Somorin

ISBN-13: 978-1-949934-67-0

Copyright © 2021 by 'Lanre Somorin, M.D.

Published by Faith 2 Fe Publishing Company
Little Rock, Arkansas 72205
www.publishyourfaith.com

Contents

DEDICATION

I dedicate this book to my late mother, Caroline Abiola Somorin. (6/25/1941–12/26/2020)

You lived a life of devotion to God and your two sons. I am thankful for the legacy of faith in God that you left us. We miss you. Continue to rest in the bosom of your Savior.

INTRODUCTION

WHAT GOD WANTS TO DO in your life is transform it. He does not want you to come out of the situation the same way you went into it. God's plan is that you thrive and excel. The Lord wants to equip you with His spiritual strength and wisdom as you walk through the changing seasons.

JAMES 1:2-4

2 My brethren, count it all joy when you fall into various trials,

3 knowing that the testing of your faith produces patience.

4 But let patience have its perfect work, that you may be perfect and complete, lacking nothing.

God will also restore the years the cankerworm has eaten (Joel 2:25). His restoration will promote you and help you move forward in life. God is not looking forward to the end of your adversity so that He can say, "Well, you made it." That would not be good enough. God wants to make sure that the adversity turns out to be a miscalculation by the enemy. In other words, if the enemy had known, he would not have messed with you.

There are certain things God wants to bring out of the adversity you are experiencing. For instance, God wants you to come out with courage. You have gone through the difficulty and you are not afraid of it anymore. You know the grace it took to get you through. Psalm 27:13 says, *"I would have lost heart, unless I had believed that I would see the goodness of the Lord in the land of the living."*

There were times when you had to encourage yourself in the Lord. You had to learn the art of self-encouragement and dig into the Word. The enemy thought he could steal your praise, but he couldn't! Satan thought he could defeat you by alienating you from other people, but you used that time to praise God more and more. If God is for you, who can be against you?

PROVERBS 18:10
10 The name of the Lord is a strong tower; The righteous run to it and are safe.

You will also come out with determination. Some people say that what doesn't kill you will make you stronger. As you traverse the changing seasons, you will learn certain things in the process, lessons you cannot learn on the mountain. Certain lessons are "valley only" lessons, which you learn when you are going through adversity.

This book will encourage you to embrace the opportunities provided by the adversity, allowing God's Word to provide a roadmap to your victory. Take each teaching into your personal time with the Lord to enlighten your perception to see yourself thriving and overcoming in every season.

Chapter One

TAKING ADVANTAGE OF OPPORTUNITIES

IN GENESIS, we find the story of Joseph, a man who was sold into slavery by his brothers. Joseph was purchased as a slave to work in the house of a man named Potiphar. The Lord was with Joseph and promoted Joseph to become the overseer of Potiphar's house.

During his time serving Potiphar, Joseph was falsely accused by Potiphar's wife, which resulted in him being placed in prison. Although Joseph was in prison, he continued to excel.

GENESIS 39:23
23 The keeper of the prison did not look into anything that was under Joseph's authority, because the Lord was with him; and whatever he did, the Lord made it prosper.

God prospered Joseph irrespective of where he was. The Lord prospered Joseph in Potiphar's house and in the prison. Even when Potiphar's wife lied about Joseph, falsely accusing him, God caused Joseph to prosper.

In this story, we see God's preparation for an event that would bring Joseph to the forefront, even while Joseph was incarcerated. Pharoah's butler and baker ended up in prison after making their leader angry. They both experienced dreams and were perplexed by what the dreams could mean for them.

GENESIS 40:1-7
1 It came to pass after these things that the butler and the baker of the king of Egypt offended their lord, the king of Egypt.

2 And Pharaoh was angry with his two officers, the chief butler and the chief baker.

3 So he put them in custody in the house of the captain of the guard, in the prison, the place where Joseph was confined.

4 And the captain of the guard charged Joseph with them, and he served them; so they were in custody for a while.

5 Then the butler and the baker of the king of Egypt, who were confined in the prison, had a dream, both of them, each man's dream in one night and each man's dream with its own interpretation.

6 And Joseph came in to them in the morning and looked at them, and saw that they were sad.

7 So he asked Pharoah's officers who were with him in the custody of his lord's house, saying, "Why do you look so sad today?"

Joseph asked each of them to describe their dreams. When the butler shared his dream, Joseph provided insight to reveal what the dream meant. It was a good dream explaining that he would be restored to favor with the Pharoah.

GENESIS 40:8-15
8 And they said to him, "We each have had a dream, and

there is no interpreter of it." So Joseph said to them, "Do not interpretations belong to God? Tell them to me, please."

9 Then the chief butler told his dream to Joseph, and said to him, "Behold, in my dream a vine was before me,

10 and in the vine were three branches; it was as though it budded, its blossoms shot forth, and its clusters brought forth ripe grapes.

11 Then Pharaoh's cup was in my hand; and I took the grapes and pressed them into Pharaoh's cup, and placed the cup in Pharaoh's hand."

12 And Joseph said to him, "This is the interpretation of it: The three branches are three days.

13 Now within three days Pharaoh will lift up your head and restore you to your place, and you will put Pharaoh's cup in his hand according to the former manner, when you were his butler.

14 But remember me when it is well with you, and please show kindness to me; make mention of me to Pharaoh, and get me out of this house.

15 For indeed I was stolen away from the land of the Hebrews; and also I have done nothing here that they should put me into the dungeon."

When Joseph interpreted the butler's dream, he asked the butler to remember him and speak to the Pharoah about him when the situation turned around. When the baker heard the favorable interpretation of the butler's dream, he also told his dream to Joseph. However, as Joseph shared the meaning of the baker's dream, it spoke of his demise.

GENESIS 40:18-23

18 So Joseph answered and said, "This is the interpretation of it: The three baskets are three days.

19 Within three days Pharaoh will lift off your head from you and hang you on a tree; and the birds will eat your flesh from you."

20 Now it came to pass on the third day, which was Pharaoh's birthday, that he made a feast for all his servants; and he lifted up the head of the chief butler and of the chief baker among his servants.

21 Then he restored the chief butler to his butlership again, and he placed the cup in Pharaoh's hand.

22 But he hanged the chief baker, as Joseph had interpreted to them.

23 Yet the chief butler did not remember Joseph, but forgot him.

Even though Joseph had asked the butler to mention him to Pharoah, he did not remember Joseph until two years later when Pharoah had a dream that disturbed him.

GENESIS 41:1
1 Then it came to pass, at the end of two full years, that Pharaoh had a dream; and behold, he stood by the river.

When Pharoah awoke from his dreams, he wanted someone to tell him what they meant. The butler remembered Joseph and how Joseph had accurately interpreted his dream.

GENESIS 41:8-13
8 Now it came to pass in the morning that his spirit was troubled, and he sent and called for all the magicians of Egypt and all its wise men. And Pharaoh told them his dreams, but there was no one who could interpret them for Pharaoh.

9 Then the chief butler spoke to Pharaoh, saying: "I remember my faults this day.

10 When Pharoah was angry with his servants, and put me in custody in the house of the captain of the guard, both me and the chief baker,

11 we each had a dream in one night, he and I. Each of us dreamed according to the interpretation of his own dream.

12 Now there was a young Hebrew man with us there, a servant of the captain of the guard. And we told him, and he interpreted our dreams for us; to each man he interpreted according to his own dream.

13 And it came to pass, just as he interpreted for us, so it happened. He restored me to my office, and he hanged him."

You may find yourself in a difficult situation like Joseph was in. Perhaps people have lied about you or said hurtful things to you. Although people may have done you wrong, you can maintain your integrity. Even if others have forgotten you, keep your heart right because God will not forget you. The Lord will raise you above the situation.

It was God's divine plan for Joseph to remain in that prison for another two years to set the stage for what would happen next. When there was a crisis, Pharaoh looked for the one who would help interpret his dream.

Crisis escalates purpose. We see that illustrated in Joseph's life. He was placed into God's plan as his community began to deal with a crisis. Just like Pharoah searched for someone who had answers to his dilemma, God will cause people to look for you.

So, this is not the time to pull back. God waited until there was a crisis and then brought Joseph to the forefront. Pharoah found Joseph, a man in whom God had placed the solution to the nation's problem. God can put the solution in you to the problems that arise in your family, company, country, state, or nation.

If you want to get to the next level, you need to be willing to solve the problems that exist in the next level. This involves recognizing and taking advantage of opportunities. One of the things I love about this story is how Joseph responded when the Pharaoh called for him.

GENESIS 41:14
14 Then Pharaoh sent and called Joseph, and they brought him quickly out of the dungeon; and he shaved, changed his clothing, and came to Pharaoh.

Joseph did not plan to return to prison. Instead, the Bible says that he shaved and changed his clothing. I want to encourage you to respond in faith. It is time to change your outlook because somebody is about to send for you.

God wants you to put a demand on yourself. Remember, that crisis will escalate purpose. God is doing something on the inside of you. Even though the plan did not come together in the first year, don't give up. You may have sent the emails and submitted the applications. Certain things that did not happen when things were good will come to pass in the time of famine. When God says this is your time, nothing can stop it except you. I want to encourage you to dress for where God is taking you. It is time to lift your head and position yourself for the next level because something is coming your way that you need to recognize.

You may have been mistreated and overlooked. You may have been doing good for all these years with no apparent progress. Then, God uses a crisis to bring you up on stage. Something good is about to happen! Embrace it, and don't let go. The future is bright, and the best is yet to come. Friend, I'm excited about what God is doing in you!

Chapter Two

BE PREPARED FOR OPPORTUNITY

AS WE GLEAN certain truths from the life of Joseph, we see how God uses an event that is a crisis to others to promote His people.

GENESIS 41:14
14 Then Pharaoh sent and called Joseph, and they brought him quickly out of the dungeon; and he shaved, changed his clothing, and came to Pharaoh.

In this text, Pharaoh called for Joseph to come out of the dungeon. But before entering the throne room of the Pharaoh, Joseph shaved and changed his clothing. This indicates a need to prepare ourselves for the next level.

GENESIS 41:15-32
15 And Pharaoh said to Joseph, "I have had a dream, and there is no one who can interpret it. But I have heard it said of you that you can understand a dream, to interpret it."

16 So Joseph answered Pharaoh, saying, "It is not in me; God will give Pharaoh an answer of peace."

17 Then Pharaoh said to Joseph: "Behold, in my dream I stood on the bank of the river.

18 Suddenly seven cows came up out of the river, fine looking and fat; and they fed in the meadow.

19 Then behold, seven other cows came up after them, poor and very ugly and gaunt, such ugliness as I have never seen in all the land of Egypt.

20 And the gaunt and ugly cows ate up the first seven, the fat cows.

21 When they had eaten them up, no one would have known that they had eaten them, for they were just as ugly as at the beginning. So I awoke.

22 Also I saw in my dream, and suddenly seven heads came up on one stalk, full and good.

23 Then behold, seven heads, withered, thin, and blighted by the east wind, sprang up after them.

24 And the thin heads devoured the seven good heads. So I told this to the magicians, but there was no one who could explain it to me."

25 Then Joseph said to Pharaoh, "The dreams of Pharaoh are one; God has shown Pharaoh what He is about to do:

26 The seven good cows are seven years, and the seven good heads are seven years; the dreams are one.

27 And the seven thin and ugly cows which came up after them are seven years, and the seven empty heads blighted by the east wind are seven years of famine.

28 This is the thing which I have spoken to Pharaoh. God has shown Pharaoh what He is about to do.

29 Indeed seven years of great plenty will come throughout all the land of Egypt;

30 but after them seven years of famine will arise, and all the plenty will be forgotten in the land of Egypt; and the famine will deplete the land.

31 So the plenty will not be known in the land because of the famine following, for it will be very severe.

32 And the dream was repeated to Pharaoh twice because the thing is established by God, and God will shortly bring it to pass.

God was trying to prepare Pharaoh for the adversity that was coming upon the nation. But there was a problem! Pharaoh could not interpret the dream from the Lord. So when Pharoah recounted the dream, Joseph used his God-given gift to interpret the dream.

Joseph didn't end his conversation after providing the interpretation. He didn't say, "Okay, may I please have an Uber to take me back to prison?" No! Joseph interpreted Pharaoh's dream and then proposed a job description. Joseph explained, "This is what you do to prepare for the seven years of famine."

GENESIS 41:33-37
33 "Now therefore, let Pharaoh select a discerning and wise man, and set him over the land of Egypt.

34 Let Pharaoh do this, and let him appoint officers over the land, to collect one-fifth of the produce of the land of Egypt in the seven plentiful years.

35 And let them gather all the food of those good years that are coming, and store up grain under the authority of Pharaoh, and let them keep food in the cities.

36 Then that food shall be as a reserve for the land for the seven years of famine which shall be in the land of Egypt, that the land may not perish during the famine.".

37 So the advice was good in the eyes of Pharaoh and in the eyes of all his servants.

God supernaturally positioned Joseph so that he could save Israel, providing Joseph the wisdom to know how to prepare against a time of famine.

There are times of plenty and times of famine. There are times when we have more and times when we may have less. It is not enough to say, "Oh, God has shown me this." We have to recognize the wisdom that God gave us to act upon in a time of adversity. God revealed what was on the horizon, but they still did not know what to do with that revelation.

Be prepared to ask God, "What should I do?" The fact that God has shown you something isn't the end of the process. You may still need to use wisdom to thrive in that situation.

By exercising his gift to interpret the dream, Joseph revealed the problem. But that alone was not sufficient. He needed to propose a solution. Some people are great at identifying the problem, but they have no idea what the solution is. They may say, "Well, yeah, this is where you missed it." Fine! But what is the solution to my situation? If God showed you something that was going to happen, it is because He wants you to prepare for it.

GENESIS 41:38
38 And Pharaoh said to his servants, "Can we find such a one as this, a man in whom is the Spirit of God?"

Do you have the Spirit of God on the inside of you? Yes! The Holy Spirit is present in every believer, and according to the Bible, Jesus has been made unto you wisdom.

1 CORINTHIANS 1:30
30 But of Him you are in Christ Jesus, who became for us wisdom from God—and righteousness and sanctification and redemption.

13

If you are saved, you have the wisdom of God inside of you. You have the mind of Christ (1 Corinthians 2:16). You have access to God's answers, plans, and strategies.

GENESIS 41:39-44

39 Then Pharaoh said to Joseph, "Inasmuch as God has shown you all this, there is no one as discerning and wise as you.

40 You shall be over my house, and all my people shall be ruled according to your word; only in regard to the throne will I be greater than you."

41 And Pharaoh said to Joseph, "See, I have set you over all the land of Egypt."

42 Then Pharaoh took his signet ring off his hand and put it on Joseph's hand; and he clothed him in garments of fine linen and put a gold chain around his neck.

43 And he had him ride in the second chariot which he had; and they cried out before him, "Bow the knee!" So he set him over all the land of Egypt.

44 Pharaoh also said to Joseph, "I am Pharaoh, and without your consent no man may lift his hand or foot in all the land of Egypt."

When Pharoah placed Joseph in command, it was a God-ordained moment! We have an example of how the crisis propelled the destiny of Joseph. God's wisdom was at work the whole time, positioning and preparing Joseph for God's plan.

You may have tried to do things your own way, but I have a better idea. According to Proverbs 3:5-6, *"Trust in the LORD with all your heart, and lean not on your own understanding; in all your ways acknowledge Him, and He shall direct your paths."* God is about to escalate His purpose in your life, even amid a crisis. This is not the time to give up or lose hope because God is positioning you for promotion.

Things seemed like they were dormant in Joseph's situation. But when the crisis hit, God positioned him, and God is going to position you too. God will give you the wisdom you need to rise from whatever prison you have encountered, whether it has been depression, a destructive relationship, financial debt, or despair.

The Bible says, *"When they cast you down, and you say, 'Exaltation will come!' Then He will save the humble person."* (Job 22:29). *"Arise, shine; for your light has come! And the glory of the LORD is risen upon you"* (Isaiah 60:1). This is not the time to draw back but the time to rise up. Your future is bright, and the Lord is your portion.

Somebody is looking for you to promote you and extend favor to you. The time for your favor is now, so be encouraged! Stay ready and be prepared because something is about to change completely.

Chapter Three

WISDOM IN A CRISIS

GOD WILL REVEAL His wisdom about adversity, providing His plan and giving us an advantage. His wisdom causes us to see from His perspective. When opportunity and crisis begin to mean the same thing to us, we will seize our moment and make the most of every opportunity.

Opportunity comes when we gain understanding and wisdom. The Bible says in Psalm 90:12, *"So teach us to number our days, that we may gain a heart of wisdom."* If we don't number our days, there is no way to gain a heart of wisdom. We must ask ourselves, "What am I meant to be doing now?"

Wisdom is required to know what we should be doing and when we should be doing them. Wisdom helps us to number our days. We should ask God to give us a heart of wisdom to recognize the things that deserve our attention. God wants us to be wiser than our situations instead of being a victim to our circumstances.

During adversity, the information on the TV is not what will benefit us. Instead, we need to align our lives with the wisdom of God. We need to know where we are in the path of life, which helps us apply wisdom to our lives.

When trouble comes, we should not hibernate to avoid the situation. Denying the problem or pretending that it doesn't exist won't help. We should search for God's wisdom, praying, "God, help me to number my days. I refuse to be distracted by the problem or enter into the hustle and bustle of adversity. What is Your Word telling me that can move me to the next level of my life?"

When we face difficult times in our lives, God's Word says we should seek wisdom.

JAMES 1:2-5

2 My brethren, count it all joy when you fall into various trials,

3 knowing that the testing of your faith produces patience.

4 But let patience have its perfect work, that you may be perfect and complete, lacking nothing.

5 If any of you lacks wisdom, let him ask of God, who gives to all liberally and without reproach, and it will be given to him.

The wisdom of God helps us to determine what is going on in our lives and how to thrive in a crisis. For instance, when we experience a trial, we are instructed to "count it all joy." If we don't understand the reason why we should "count it all joy," we should ask God for His wisdom.

God's Word says we should seek wisdom, but wisdom is often the last thing people seek when they are confronted with a bad situation. Most people just want to escape. They don't want to learn how they got themselves into that situation or what to do to prevent it from happening again. Obviously, no two situations are the same, but there is always something to learn from every crisis.

In a time of shortage, you may ask yourself, "How many of those things do I really need?". You may look at your relationship with your spouse and say, "Wow! I have been neglecting my marriage. I haven't really invested in my spouse or my family." In seasons when you find yourself alone, you can ask, "What does this teach me about myself?"

Even though we desire to come out of the difficulty, we need the wisdom of God to develop patience. When everything is good, you don't have the same opportunity to develop patience. But in a crisis, you have that opportunity.

The Bible says that the trying of your faith helps you to develop patience. But the crisis won't develop patience if you don't ask God for wisdom. Patience is a spiritual staying power that is a vital part of your faith.

HEBREWS 6:12
12 That you do not become sluggish, but imitate those who through faith and patience inherit the promises.

Patience is so important—especially in a crisis. Often, we just want the problem to go away. We say, "When is it going to end?" Yes, we want it to end, but we cannot determine the exact date it will end. We must be patient and continue confessing and standing upon the Word of God. God will help us to bring the crisis to an end.

If we are facing a problem, we need to figure out what we can learn from it because we can learn from every adversity and be better prepared in the future. We want to learn from it to ensure that we are not repeating the same cycle over and over again. Christ is in us and has become our wisdom. We must tap into that wisdom.

God once told me, "Somebody, somewhere, is planning your future." I believe that is true for you today. Somebody somewhere is saying, "Wow! This is how we are going to reorganize things on this job." You need to be in the planning mode, not just waiting for somebody to hand something over to you. You may not like what they hand to you. Instead, be engaged in the process.

God wants us to use His wisdom in times of crisis. So, choose to seek the wisdom of God. Wisdom is vital because it will position us for what will happen next in God's plan and help us maintain patience.

Chapter Four

ARE YOU PREPARED FOR CHANGE?

DAVID WAS SENT to take supplies to his brothers who were on the battlefield. The armies were confronted daily with threats from Goliath. For about 40 days, there had been a standstill as Goliath taunted them, saying, *"Give me a man, that we may fight together"* (1 Samuel 17:10). But there was no one among the armies of Israel willing to fight him.

David arrived on the battlefield and heard the soldiers asking, *"Have you seen this man who has come up?"*

1 SAMUEL 17:25
25 So the men of Israel said, "Have you seen this man who has come up? Surely he has come up to defy Israel; and it shall be that the man who kills him the king will enrich with great riches, will give him his daughter, and give his father's house exemption from taxes in Israel."

David perceived this attack as an opportunity and responded with a question of his own.

1 SAMUEL 17:26-27
26 Then David spoke to the men who stood by him, saying, "What shall be done for the man who kills this Philistine and takes away the reproach from Israel? For who is this uncircumcised Philistine, that he should defy the armies of the living God?"

27 And the people answered him in this manner, saying, "So shall it be done for the man who kills him."

While David was concerned about the reproach that Goliath was bringing on the nation, he also wanted clarification about the recompense he would receive when he removed the reproach. For David, the crisis and the opportunity were connected.

Many times, God brings opportunity out of the crisis. When you look back at your life at some of the most significant opportunities, you may discover that it didn't look like an opportunity at the onset. It appeared to be adversity.

As we believe God for the difficulty to end, we begin to walk by faith and not by sight. Instead of waiting for the problem to end, we begin to plan for it to come to an end.

If you are planning a wedding, you don't just wait for that day to come. Many of the preparations must be made in advance. The same is true concerning your breakthrough.

When you find yourself in a crisis, begin to make your exit preparations. *"The thief does not come except to steal, and to kill, and to destroy. I have come that they may have life, and that they may have it more abundantly."* (John 10:10). Let's make our preparations, saying, "I'm coming out with greater than anything the enemy may have pictured for my life. It is not just a matter of coming out by the skin of my teeth. I am coming out stronger!"

We must have more than a short-term focus. To accomplish this, we have to cultivate our expectations. Don't allow your mind to be bombarded with the negatives of the situation. Instead, celebrate the positives. For example, I once had a conversation with a friend, discussing an opportunity. I asked, "What do you think of this opportunity?"

She countered with a question, "Well, what is your vision?"

I answered, "I am not trying to talk about where I plan to be in 15 years right now. I'm just telling you about this opportunity that came up. You know, just give me your thoughts on it.

She asked me again, "Well, what is your vision? Eventually, I got annoyed and gave her a brief answer. Later, she explained, "At some point, you must switch from making decisions based on a short-term vision, saying, "This opportunity is good for now. Let me do it."

There are times when you must look a couple of years down the line and ask, "What am I doing today to position myself in the vision I have for my future? It is more than just thinking about survival or what is good for this moment."

She made an excellent point. This conversation led me to the following illustration: If somebody calls you and says, "I'm at this intersection, and I'm really wondering whether to make a left or right turn. The first question you will ask is, "Where are you? The next question is, "Where are you going?

In my first book, *Seize Your Moment: Unmasking Everyday Opportunities,* I explained that you need to stop having a short-term vision for your life and think of the long-term impact of the decisions you make today. So, what can you do today to help position yourself for the future?

PROVERBS 16:1
1 The preparations of the heart belong to man, but the answer of the tongue is from the LORD.

God leaves the preparation to man. The Lord will not prepare for you. Benjamin Franklin said, "By failing to prepare, you are preparing to fail."[1] Whether your goal is to improve your health, financial position, academic standing, career, or relationships with your family, you must prepare. Preparation takes planning. It involves recognizing where you are and where you want to be. Preparation requires that you know what tools you need to reach your desired destination and the order in which you must acquire the tools. Start preparing today for tomorrow's opportunities.

At the beginning of a race, they say, "Ready. Set. Go!" The people who took their mark and made themselves ready to run will be prepared for the command to "GO!" The Lord wants us to prepare for opportunities even in a crisis, praying and trusting in Him to give us wisdom and direction, asking Him, "What are the next steps? What do I need to do to position myself?

William Ward said, "Men never plan to be failures; they simply fail to plan to be successful."[2]

How are you planning? What do you need to do to plan? How do you need to position yourself?

John Mason mentioned, "Few know when to rise to the occasion. Most only know when to sit down."[3]

What are you going to do to prepare for the opportunities God is bringing your way this year? You have prayed for open doors and opportunities, but what are you going to do to position yourself to take advantage of those opportunities?

ISAIAH 1:19
19 If you are willing and obedient, you shall eat the good of the land.

Now is the time to be willing and obedient, but it starts with preparation. You don't want to look back a year from now, saying, "Well, I really wish I had made better use of my time."This is the time to dig into God's Word and discover what plans He has for your life. Position yourself to seek God. Through preparation, you can maximize your opportunity.

Chapter Five

WAIT ON THE LORD AND BE OF GOOD COURAGE

IN THE MIDDLE of difficulty, we must stand on the Word of God, establishing our heart on God's covenant.

PSALM 27:13-14

13 I would have lost heart, unless I had believed that I would see the goodness of the Lord in the land of the living.

14 Wait on the Lord; Be of good courage, and He shall strengthen your heart; Wait, I say, on the Lord!

Sometimes we may not recognize the difference between what we know and the things we are exposed to in life. If we are going to make a positive difference, we must guard our hearts. We have to figure out how God wants us to pray and how He wants us to respond.

Constantly exposing our hearts to the details of the crisis could overwhelm us because we are not built to function that way. While we need to be aware of what is going on around us, we also need to be able to pray. If we are overwhelmed by adversity, our hearts will not be in a condition to pray. David said that he would have lost heart unless he had believed that he would see the goodness of the Lord in the land of the living.

People will argue their need to focus on the statistics and details of their problems. They say, "What are we to do if we aren't focused on all of this?" The Bible instructs us to wait on the Lord.

PSALM 27:14
14 Wait on the Lord; Be of good courage, and He shall strengthen your heart; Wait, I say, on the Lord!

Courage doesn't come by wishing. Our hearts develop courage as we are waiting on the Lord. What does it mean to "wait on the Lord?" One way is by meditating upon the Word of God. Instead of discussing the problem, you can rehearse the goodness of God, talking about His goodness to your friends and family. In Psalm 27:1, we see this declaration, *"The LORD is my light and my salvation; Whom shall I fear? The LORD is the strength of my life; Of whom shall I be afraid?"* David had been waiting on the Lord, meditating on His faithfulness. The Word of God created a picture of courage, rescue, and salvation.

Waiting on the Lord involves speaking the Word of God over your life, over your situation, and recognizing that the Lord is your portion. Don't lose heart because of what is going on around you. Instead, believe that you will see the goodness of the Lord in the land of the living.

Are you waiting on the Lord, or are you waiting on the adversity? If you're waiting on the adversity, it will fill your heart with fear, causing you to lose heart. But if you wait on the Lord, you will be of good courage, and God will strengthen your heart. Then, you will be able to pray for those who need prayer and encourage those who need encouragement. You can be a blessing to somebody. So, what are you waiting for?

PROVERBS 13:12
12 Hope deferred makes the heart sick, but when the desire comes, it is a tree of life.

In other words, you wish that the trial would end, but each time you defer your hope, it causes depression. Hope that is deferred makes the heart sick. So, don't defer your hope. Just choose to wait upon the Lord! This is a daily activity of meditating on Him. This is not a sprint but a marathon.

If you say, "Well, I can tolerate this for a week," but the difficulty continues for four weeks, you need to change your focus. Stop deferring your hope to a certain date and time and stop attaching a due date to your hope. Instead, simply wait on the Lord and be of good courage. He will strengthen your heart, and strength is what we need.

Chapter Six

ENCOURAGE YOURSELF IN THE LORD

DAVID USED HIS experience with the lion and the bear to develop confidence that God would come through for him. As a result, he gained the boldness to face Goliath. One of the remarkable things about David is that when God did something for him, David always responded with a song. When he was sad, he sang a song, and when he was happy, he sang a song. When the battle ended in victory, David sang a song.

PSALM 118:14
14 The Lord is my strength and song, And He has become my salvation.

Sometimes the victory is not in your understanding—it is in your song. You don't have to understand things to be able to sing. When looking back at what God has done for you, remind yourself of God's goodness in your life and worship Him. In a difficult season, you should not lose your song.

A few years ago, during a worship service in the church I attend, God spoke the following instruction: "You came into this year singing, and you are going to come out singing. But make sure that nothing steals your song." For many people, they enter the season singing but misplace their song during the hard times. You can come out of the adversity singing!

The Lord God is your strength and song. In other words, there is strength in song. The Scriptures provide multiple examples of times when God used the praises of His people to deliver them. It was not their swords or their mighty armies but their praise.

I want to emphasize the role of praising God because being grounded by praise is crucial.

PSALM 89:15-16
15 Blessed are the people who know the joyful sound! They walk, O Lord, in the light of Your countenance.

16 In Your name they rejoice all day long, and in Your righteousness they are exalted.

* * *

PSALM 89:15-16 MSG
15 Blessed are the people who know the passwords of praise, who shout on parade in the bright presence of God.

16 Delighted, they dance all day long; they know who you are, what you do—they can't keep it quiet!

There is a password that is needed—the password of praise. You may not understand what is going on around you, but you don't need to understand to be able to praise

God. The Bible says, *"Let everything that has breath praise the LORD. Praise the LORD!"* (Psalm 150:6).

God's Word instructs us, *"In everything give thanks; for this is the will of God in Christ Jesus for you."* (1 Thessalonians 5:18).

Don't allow the circumstances to steal your praise. On the contrary, put your praise into high gear! Praise is one of the weapons of your warfare. The Bible says that we should put on the garment of praise for the spirit of heaviness (Isaiah 61:3). Victory is not found by examining or thinking about the spirit of heaviness. You must put on something new, put on praise. Throw open the blinds and put on praise songs that will help you remember the goodness of God.

That is part of God's preparation for a season of trial. He may have put a song in your heart months or even years ago. You need to get that song out and begin to sing it because it will turn your heart back to God. The worship will help you to put God in perspective and turn your focus to the goodness of God.

On your phone, you may have some songs in your playlist for driving, exercising, or just relaxing. But you need to create another playlist for battle. If the songs on your playlist don't motivate you, you need to change them and get some battle songs. The Bible says the Lord is my strength and my song and has become my salvation. Your song will help to take you through the storm. What song are you singing?

Don't let anything steal your praise. Remember the password of praise. Blessed are the people who know that joyful sound because they will walk in the light of God's countenance. God will give you wisdom and direction as you praise Him. He will provide strategies as you are praising. God will defeat your enemies, pushing back darkness, depression, and heaviness as you put on the garment of praise.

This is not the time to say, "Well, I can't. How am I going to praise God without the choir?"

David encouraged himself in the Lord, and you can be your own one-man band! You can have your own praise party right there in your house. Encourage yourself in the Lord and create an atmosphere of praise in your home. It will help you to walk in victory. *The Lord is my strength and song, and He has become my salvation* (Psalm 118:14).

Chapter Seven

IT MAY BE UNEXPECTED, BUT YOU ARE NOT UNPREPARED

ONE DAY, AS I AWOKE, the Lord quickened this statement to me, "It may be unexpected, but you are not unprepared." God has prepared you for the season you are experiencing.

Somebody might ask, "How?" One of the key preparations is found in this text from Hebrews 13:

HEBREWS 13:5-6 AMPC
5 Let your character or moral disposition be free from love of money [including greed, avarice, lust, and craving for earthly possessions] and be satisfied with your present [circumstances and with what you have]; for He [God] Himself has said, I will not in any way fail you nor give you up nor leave you without support. [I will] not, [I will] not, [I will] not in any degree leave you helpless nor forsake nor let [you] down (relax My hold on you)! [Assuredly not!]

6 So we take comfort and are encouraged and confidently and boldly say, The Lord is my Helper; I will not be seized

with alarm [I will not fear or dread or be terrified]. What can man do to me?

God said that He would never leave us nor forsake us. He will not under any circumstances desert us, give us up, or leave us without support. God will not in any degree leave us helpless. God is always with us!

Before the accessibility of GPS technology, we needed a map to travel into unfamiliar places. I remember when you could go online and download the directions because there were no GPS systems available. But the map didn't help if you encountered construction or serious traffic. You had to figure out how to reroute around the accident or construction. If you were depending on the map, you had to pray that nothing unexpected would happen!

With GPS, it is real-time! If there is congestion or traffic, the GPS will recalculate and reroute you. The GPS is making those adjustments for you and giving you an estimated time of arrival. It has already factored in other unexpected things that could happen down the line.

If the GPS that is man-made could accomplish these things, how much more will God, through His Holy Spirit on the inside of us, provide course corrections for our lives. He will never leave us nor forsake us. If we are connected to God's GPS, He provides the light on our path and the lamp to our feet when we encounter unexpected events. The Lord is there to reroute us so that we arrive at the destination God has planned for us.

JEREMIAH 29:11
11 For I know the thoughts that I think toward you, says the LORD, thoughts of peace and not of evil, to give you a future and a hope.

On occasion, I followed the turn-by-turn directions of my GPS that took me through some dangerous areas. But as long as I was connected to the signal on the GPS, I had confidence. Even when I was in the woods, far out in the country, or driving through a dangerous part of town, I knew the GPS was connected to a source of information far above where I was. I assured myself that I was directed by a satellite that was up in the heavens.

Well, we have a heavenly satellite located inside of us. Even though unexpected things come our way, God said He would never leave us nor forsake us. The Lord will not relax His hold on us, so we can maintain our connection with Him during difficult times.

One thing that has been beneficial for me is to look back at the truths the Lord has taught me. I revisit the words that God has already spoken to me in the past. As I do, I realize that God had been laying a foundation by revealing things to me in advance. He developed my faith, patience, and joy before the crisis began. When I was in school, I didn't know when the test would come so I had to stay prepared. Don't let your heart fail because of an unexpected crisis. God is on the inside of you.

God, the Holy Spirit, is our Waymaker. He makes a way where there seems to be no way and will help you navigate your path. Don't try to live by the old map you downloaded years ago. You may have encountered something unexpected, but the Holy Spirit is rerouting you. He is letting you know that He factored the adversity into His calculations. As a result, He will lead you to the expected end.

Our responsibility is to stay connected to His GPS. Don't disconnect like Peter did while walking on water. As long as Peter held onto what Jesus said, he continued to walk on water. It may be unexpected, but you are not unprepared. *"But when he saw that the wind was boisterous, he was afraid; and beginning to sink..."* (Matt. 14:30). We need to hold onto the Word of God and let the Lord navigate us through the unexpected because God has prepared the way for us.

It may be unexpected to you, but it is not unexpected to your divine GPS. The natural GPS can factor in the problems and, within seconds, tell you what the fastest route is to take. How much more has God factored in the plans of the enemy and prepared a path of victory? The Lord has navigated you through murky waters for years and years. He will never leave you helpless, so you can confidently and boldly say, "The Lord is my Helper! I will not fear what man will do to me" (Heb. 13:6).

Chapter Eight

GOD'S DELIVERING POWER DOES NOT CHANGE

GOD USED A NATIONAL CRISIS to accelerate purpose in the life of David. David perceived Goliath as a door to a new beginning. We know this to be true because David had already asked about the reward that would be given to the man who killed Goliath in 1 Samuel 17:26.

Also, God used the crisis to bring David out of obscurity. David had been in the wilderness, but God used the situation to get him to the forefront. When it comes to a crisis, the title or position is not the determining factor. Boldness and courage are the currency in a crisis.

1 SAMUEL 17:32-35
32 Then David said to Saul, "Let no man's heart fail because of him; your servant will go and fight with this Philistine."

33 And Saul said to David, "You are not able to go against this Philistine to fight with him; for you are a youth, and he a man of war from his youth."

34 But David said to Saul, "Your servant used to keep his father's sheep, and when a lion or a bear came and took a lamb out of the flock,

35 I went out after it and struck it, and delivered the lamb from its mouth; and when it arose against me, I caught it by its beard, and struck and killed it.

David recounted his victory over the lion and the bear. His confidence that he will defeat Goliath in the same way is displayed in his testimony.

While the Israelites perceived Goliath and his threats as the end of their lives as they knew it, David saw it as a door to a new beginning. Crisis can be a door to a new beginning for you if you maintain the right perception. What others see as an obstacle can be the thing that causes you to come out of the wilderness, out of obscurity, to where God wants you to be. A crisis can accelerate purpose in your life and cause courage and boldness to rise in your heart, moving you into what God has in store for you.

King Saul thought David was not qualified to fight Goliath. He told David, *"for you are a youth, and he a man of war from his youth."* But David made it clear that God's delivering power did not change based on the size of the enemy. He rehearsed his previous victories and declared that God would deliver him from the hand of the Philistine too!

First, David trusted in his delivering God. Second, David rehearsed how God had delivered him in the past.

You and I can do the same thing! Instead of allowing the negative circumstances to overwhelm us, we can remember what God delivered us from in times past.

David wrote many songs describing how God had delivered him. Those songs helped him maintain the memories of the victories. What song do you have in your heart?

In the middle of adversity, remember God's prior deliverances. Rehearse every time when God has brought you out on top. You don't need a choir or a scheduled testimony service at church. Instead, pull out those songs of victory and remind yourself of the God that you serve.

The third thing that we see in this example is that David realized the covenant he had with God was greater than the opposition presented by Goliath.

> **1 SAMUEL 17:36-37**
> **36 Your servant has killed both lion and bear; and this uncircumcised Philistine will be like one of them, seeing he has defied the armies of the living God."**
>
> **37 Moreover David said, "The LORD, who delivered me from the paw of the lion and from the paw of the bear, He will deliver me from the hand of this Philistine." And Saul said to David, "Go, and the LORD be with you!"**

David knew that anyone who threatened the covenant, God would defeat. David's covenant with God gave him the advantage because whoever came against David was not just coming against him. They were coming against David *and* God! In David's mind, his victory was already settled!

The term "uncircumcised" used in verse 36, refers to the fact that Goliath was not in covenant with God because circumcision was a sign or symbol of the covenant. David based his confidence on the fact that he was in covenant with God and Goliath wasn't. Only those who had a covenant with God would still be standing at the end of the battle.

Whatever situation you are facing, whether it is depression, unemployment, or trouble in your marriage, you need to recognize that it falls under the category of "uncircumcised." You have a covenant with God that guarantees victory in any situation, so don't let your heart fail. Your covenant is greater than the situation. Even though the armies had been confronted with Goliath for at least 40 days before David showed up on the scene, David did not allow the duration of the attack or the intensity of the adversity to distract him from the power of God's covenant.

DANIEL 11:32
32 Those who do wickedly against the covenant he shall corrupt with flattery; but the people who know their God shall be strong, and carry out great exploits.

David is a wonderful example of what is revealed in Daniel 11:32. He knew God and relied on his covenant with the Lord. You and I can also demonstrate this spiritual strength. We must remind ourselves that our covenant is with Him. This is a time to be strong in our knowledge of the covenant because that knowledge enables us to rise above the circumstances and do exploits.

The same God who gave David victory over the bear and the lion will deliver us from whatever comes against us. His delivering power does not change because of the size of our enemy.

The covenant we have is greater than the opposition. God's power is still in effect, and the people who know their God shall be strong and do exploits. This is the season for you to get deep into your covenant with God and know that nothing is greater than your covenant. Go ahead and be strong and do exploits in Jesus' name.

Chapter Nine

YOU ARE THE SOLUTION IN A CRISIS

WE SEE MANY EXAMPLES in the Scriptures where God used a crisis to accelerate purpose. Even when it wasn't something they were expecting, God knew that the crisis would come and prepared them for it.

Don't lose sight of what God has in store for you. You will make it through this adversity stronger than you were before because God's plan for you is good.

JEREMIAH 29:11
11 For I know the thoughts that I think toward you, says the LORD, thoughts of peace and not of evil, to give you a future and a hope.

I like to say, "If it is not expected, it is not the end because your end is going to be expected." Keep looking for God's plan and move in the direction of what He has spoken.

David's brother asked him, "Who is feeding the sheep in the wilderness?" In other words, he was telling David, "You are meant to be in obscurity."

1 SAMUEL 17:25-29

25 So the men of Israel said, "Have you seen this man who has come up? Surely he has come up to defy Israel; and it shall be that the man who kills him the king will enrich with great riches, will give him his daughter, and give his father's house exemption from taxes in Israel."

26 Then David spoke to the men who stood by him, saying, "What shall be done for the man who kills this Philistine and takes away the reproach from Israel? For who is this uncircumcised Philistine, that he should defy the armies of the living God?"

27 And the people answered him in this manner, saying, "So shall it be done for the man who kills him."

28 Now Eliab his oldest brother heard when he spoke to the men; and Eliab's anger was aroused against David, and he said, "Why did you come down here? And with whom have you left those few sheep in the wilderness? I know your pride and the insolence of your heart, for you have come down to see the battle."

29 And David said, "What have I done now? Is there not a cause?"

Be willing to step out of obscurity, whether it is in your company, organization, or with your friends. There is something in you that is needed to overcome the crisis, but you will have to move past the limits and expectations of other people.

As believers, our access to God's wisdom, peace, and joy is of immense value. When there is no adversity, people underestimate the value of joy, peace, and contentment. But if we maintain our cool when other people are falling apart, people will notice. We have an opportunity to let people know the key to our peace and victory.

The joy of the Lord strengthens us. Our composure is a result of the Person Who abides in us. Sometimes, people say, "Well, let's keep hope alive." Actually, we have a Living Hope! We have resurrection life on the inside of us.

Saul was the king but his title didn't give him the advantage. A title or position is not as important in a crisis as having courage. David had courage, and that courage was of greater value than the title of king or even the king's armor. Boldness is a currency in a time of crisis.

So don't say, "Well, I don't have the title, so I really cannot step up on my job or step up in the situation." It doesn't matter what your title is when you have a covenant with God. You have a gift to give! There is something in you that can overcome the crisis! So, stop being a silent observer, just absorbing the news. Instead, you need to ask God, "What have you deposited in me that is for this crisis?"

God can cause the limitations that may have prevented you from stepping into purpose to be removed. God is bringing you out of obscurity and accelerating purpose, so this is not the time to throw away what God has placed on the inside of you.

God will use a crisis to bring you out of obscurity. Proverbs 18:16 says, *A man's gift makes room for him, and brings him before great men.."* It is time to dust off your uniform because you are coming out of obscurity.

Boldness is the currency in a crisis—not the title or position. So be encouraged because God has not given you the spirit of fear but of power, love, and a sound, well-balanced mind (2 Timothy 1:7). Let your light shine because this is your season. God is aware of what is going on and has equipped you for this. You are the solution to an evolving crisis.

Chapter Ten

DON'T LET YOUR PREFERENCE KEEP YOU FROM YOUR PROMISE

GOD'S PLAN FOR YOU is still on schedule. God will give you a promise and speak to you about the end of the matter. However, the Lord doesn't necessarily give us the full details of what will happen in the process leading up to the end.

Often, we receive the promise from God and become excited. Then, a month or two later, we hit a roadblock. We may say, "I'm not sure if God saw this coming." The Lord definitely saw it coming and already had a plan to overcome it. Unfortunately, we tend to retreat and say, "Well, God did not really factor this into the picture."

In my book, *Seize Your Moment: Unmasking Everyday Opportunities,* I taught that the story of David and

Goliath illustrates how opportunity comes in the midst of adversity.

Goliath stood on the battlefield, taunting the armies of the Israelites for about 40 days. David was sent to deliver food for his brothers in battle when he overheard the soldiers talking about the recompense for the person who could defeat Goliath.

> **1 SAMUEL 17:25-27**
> **25 So the men of Israel said, "Have you seen this man who has come up? Surely he has come up to defy Israel; and it shall be that the man who kills him the king will enrich with great riches, will give him his daughter, and give his father's house exemption from taxes in Israel."**
>
> **26 Then David spoke to the men who stood by him, saying, "What shall be done for the man who kills this Philistine and takes away the reproach from Israel? For who is this uncircumcised Philistine, that he should defy the armies of the living God?"**
>
> **27 And the people answered him in this manner, saying, "So shall it be done for the man who kills him."**

David saw the adversity as an opportunity to find a spouse, be made rich, and be set free from paying taxes. That is why he kept asking, *"What shall be done to the man that kills this Philistine...?"* The Israelites perceived Goliath as being the end of life as they knew it, but David saw Goliath as an opportunity for his breakthrough. David looked beyond the situation to what would happen after Goliath. He focused on the victory instead of visualizing defeat.

The "Goliath" in your life could come in the form

of a job that places a demand on you, a family problem, or a crisis. Your victory is on the other side of the fear associated with the problem. When God gives an instruction, fear shows up. But you must hold on to what God is saying. You cannot allow fear to keep you from the promises of God.

David focused on what was going to happen after Goliath's defeat. One of the things that I like in this story is David's response after being questioned by his brother.

1 SAMUEL 17:29
29 And David said, "What have I done now? Is there not a cause?"

Begin to look at your promise intently. It could be something that will push you into your destiny. David was anointed as king in Chapter 16, but Goliath was the opportunity that opened the path to the throne. We need to have the same mindset as David that looks beyond to see what will be done for the person who slays Goliath.

You might possess the wisdom to solve the problem your company is facing. You may be in a unique position to meet certain needs in your community. It may not be something that grabs you at first, but God wants to use your gift to be a blessing to somebody. It can start right where you are by using your gift to be a blessing.

God said to me, "Don't let your preference keep you

from your promise." Things may have changed, and they may not be your preference. But don't let it keep you from your promise. Whether it is something new that God is doing or if God resurrects something that you have put aside, God will escalate, shift, and accelerate you into the purpose. You can boldly declare, "I am not coming out of this empty. I'm going to thrive in this crisis. I am coming out boldly with a fresh vision. God is making things even clearer to me." You need to ask yourself, "Is there not a cause?"

Just like David was focused on what would be done for the person who defeated Goliath, you can look ahead to the reward. Your victory is on the other side of your fear. Don't let fear stop you. Instead, push beyond the fear and embrace the purposes of God for your life. This is your season and time to rise up and slay your Goliath because there is a cause. That cause is going to move you to your next level.

Chapter Eleven

GOD'S PURPOSE FOR YOU IS STILL ON SCHEDULE

JEREMIAH 29:11 in *The Amplified Bible Classic Edition* says, *"For I know the thoughts and plans that I have for you, says the Lord, thoughts and plans for welfare and peace and not for evil, to give you hope in your final outcome."* God's purpose for your life is still on schedule. His plans for you are to give you a future and hope.

You may have anticipated the great things God has in store only to be distracted by the plans of the enemy to bring devastation. Keep your focus on God's desire for your life because you are established in the righteousness of God.

ISAIAH 54:13-14 AMPC
13 And all thy children shall be taught of the Lord; and great shall be the peace of thy children.

14 You shall establish yourself in righteousness (rightness, in conformity with God's will and order): you shall be far

**from even the thought of oppression or destruction, for you
shall not fear, and from terror, for it shall not come near you.**

When we know we are righteous, it establishes us
firm against the enemy's attacks. Proverbs 28:1 says,
*"The wicked flee when no one pursues, but the righteous are
bold as a lion."*

We are the righteousness of God in Christ Jesus.
Righteousness has nothing to do with the church that you
attend. It has to do with your relationship with Christ. We
have been made the righteousness of God in Christ Jesus
(2 Corinthians 5:21). The Bible says that in
righteousness, you shall be established. You will be far
from oppression because you shall not fear. You will be
far from terror, for it will not come near you.

ISAIAH 54:15-17
**15 Indeed they shall surely assemble, but not because of Me.
Whoever assembles against you shall fall for your sake.**

**16 "Behold, I have created the blacksmith who blows the
coals in the fire, who brings forth an instrument for his
work; and I have created the spoiler to destroy.**

**17 No weapon formed against you shall prosper, and every
tongue which rises against you in judgment you shall
condemn. This is the heritage of the servants of the LORD,
and their righteousness is from Me," says the LORD.**

The enemy is still hoping to take you out, but none
of his weapons will be able to stand. We can believe
God for overall protection over our lives and our mental
health. Some weapons will come against your thoughts,
saying, "This is the end." You need to condemn those
thoughts and cast them down. You are the righteousness

of God in Christ Jesus, and in righteousness, you will be established.

No weapon formed against you will be able to prosper. So, don't be overwhelmed by the weapon, the issue. It is not going to prosper. You have a heritage of victory. Speak the Word. Recognize that God is still on schedule with everything He promised you. The thief comes to steal, kill, and destroy, but Jesus came that we might have life and have it more abundantly (John 10:10). God's purpose towards you is still on schedule, so don't be moved off His schedule.

Chapter Twelve

THE REAL QUESTION IS "WHO IS LOVING YOU?"

ROMANS 8:31-32, 35-37
31 What then shall we say to these things? If God is for us, who can be against us?

32 He who did not spare His own Son, but delivered Him up for us all, how shall He not with Him also freely give us all things?

35 Who shall separate us from the love of Christ? Shall tribulation, or distress, or persecution, or famine, or nakedness, or peril, or sword?

36 As it is written: "For Your sake we are killed all day long; We are accounted as sheep for the slaughter."

37 Yet in all these things we are more than conquerors through Him who loved us.

If I were to ask you, "What is the biggest thing going on in your life today?" how would you respond? Most people respond with a detailed description of their difficulties. But the most significant thing happening in your life is not the problem that is coming your way. It is the love of God towards you! The love of God towards you is unchanged, and as we see in the verse mentioned above, *"...in all these things we are more than conquerors through him that loved us."*

ROMANS 8:38-39
38 For I am persuaded that neither death nor life, nor angels nor principalities nor powers, nor things present nor things to come,

39 nor height nor depth, nor any other created thing, shall be able to separate us from the love of God which is in Christ Jesus our Lord.

The Bible declares that none of these adverse situations can separate us from the love of God. In other words, the love of God is so powerful that it is greater than any negative circumstance that will come against you. Therefore, we need to major in the love of God.

The Bible says we are more than conquerors. Regardless of the crisis, it is not big enough to separate us from the love of God. You may have said, "Well, the headache is not big enough to separate me," or "My boss is not big enough to separate me." You have no problem believing that the common, day-to-day problems are no match for the love of God.

But what about something that is not common adversity? What about something that may come once in a generation like the Covid-19 pandemic? Are those types of problems included in the things that cannot separate you from the love of God?

In times of adversity, you may ask, "Where am I placing my trust?" If your trust is in the government, a CEO, your local officials, etc., you may lose confidence. Although they try to do their best, they don't have it all under control. So, if your trust is in the government, an institution, or a person, it won't be stable.

God is our source, and His love toward us is alive and active. The issue is not what we are going through, but Who is loving us. If our trust is in a person, they have limits in their ability to protect and lead us. But the love of God toward us is unchanged, and nothing can separate us from that love.

We can develop in our confidence about the love of God to the point that we say, *"I am persuaded...."* We can move from the point of "knowing" to being "persuaded." This is not the time to shrink back from the love of God. As believers, we should be experts in knowing and understanding the power of His love. We are ambassadors of God's love!

A crisis tends to bring out the best and the worst in people. For example, when the Covid-19 pandemic occurred, people began to hoard hand sanitizer and toilet paper. The price went up, and it reached a point where you couldn't even find them. Others were hoarding the things that people needed during that difficult time. What an opportunity to be an ambassador of the love of God.

My question to you today is: "Who is loving you?" Jesus loves you and is telling you that because of His love, you are more than a conqueror. No matter the situation, nothing can separate you from the love of God. Don't try to be your own protector because God is your protector and the source of your peace. He has protected you from many things that could have destroyed you.

Jesus' love toward you is the greatest thing going on in your life right now. His love is bigger than your problems and makes you more than a conqueror. Are you persuaded? I want to encourage you to major in the love of God. Don't spend all your time focused on the crisis because you need to be persuaded about God's love, not the problem. God's love for you is steadfast, and it is the biggest thing going on in your life right now.

If you don't know Christ as your Lord and Savior, this is the time to come to Him. Jesus is still saving today, and if you don't know Him, pray this prayer to invite Jesus into your life:

Father, in the name of Jesus, I thank you for sending Jesus to be my Lord. I accept Jesus into my life as my Lord and Savior. Forgive me of all my sins. I believe that Jesus died on the cross and that He rose again from the dead. I confess Jesus with my mouth today as my Lord and Savior. Jesus, come into my life and save me. Amen

The Bible says that with the heart man believes,

and with the mouth confession is made unto salvation (Romans 10:10). If you prayed that prayer and believed it, you now have a relationship with Jesus Christ. Find a good, Bible-believing church to attend so you can become persuaded in the love God has toward you.

Chapter Thirteen

THE LORD IS YOUR PORTION

LAMENTATIONS 3:21-23

21 This I recall to my mind, therefore I have hope.

22 Through the LORD's mercies we are not consumed, because His compassions fail not.

23 They are new every morning; great is Your faithfulness.

EVEN THOUGH WE NEED to be informed about what is going on, it is more important to recall what God *has done* in our lives. Remember and rehearse the times God has brought you through difficult situations, health scares, financial difficulties, or hard times in your family or job.

Our God is a miracle-working God, and I have good news for you. This is not His rookie year! He did not get into the deliverance business recently. God is a God of a thousand generations. He is a God Who heals and saves.

But we need to recall God's goodness, especially in times of difficulty, because it is through the Lord's mercies that we are not consumed. His compassions fail not. It wasn't your goodness that has kept you alive up until now but the Lord's mercies.

God's compassion and mercies are new every morning. It is not the alarm on your phone that woke you up this morning. It was God's goodness! God's goodness is what has preserved us, and nothing has changed regarding His goodness.

During the Covid-19 pandemic, we were told to practice social distancing. But God is not practicing social distancing. He is near! In James 4:8, the Bible says, *"Draw near to God and He will draw near to you."*

The same God Who has brought you through difficult situations is still there for you, and His mercies are new every morning. Each new day triggers a new grace and new mercy. Sometimes people say, "Well, it is a new day with all of the old problems." No! God's mercy is restocked, refreshed, and newly activated every day. So hold on to that mercy! Major on the mercy and the goodness of God.

LAMENTATIONS 3:24-26
24 "The LORD is my portion," says my soul, "Therefore I hope in Him!"

25 The LORD is good to those who wait for Him, to the soul who seeks Him.

26 It is good that one should hope and wait quietly for the salvation of the LORD.

During a crisis, you really need to know that the Lord is your portion. No matter what is going on, Psalm 91:7 says, *"A thousand may fall at your side, and ten thousand at your right hand; but it shall not come near you."* As a child of God, the Bible has identified that the Lord is your portion. You are not without help or hope because God is your portion.

You must hold on to the consolation that God's mercies are new every morning. Don't allow your heart to be overwhelmed by the symptoms or the report of the problem because you need your heart to be in a condition to receive from God. You need to be in a spiritual condition to pray, be a blessing, and reach out to people. You need to be spiritually strong so that you can fulfill God's purpose concerning your life. God is not on "pause." He has not stopped ministering to people. God is alive, and He is your portion.

Expose your heart to the Word of God every day. The Word of God is the diet of the believer, and a difficult time is not the time to change your diet. Actually, your diet of God's Word may mean the difference between life and death.

PSALM 119:92
92 Unless Your law had been my delight, I would then have perished in my affliction.

PSALM 119:111
111 Your testimonies I have taken as a heritage forever, for they are the rejoicing of my heart.

There are many sources of information on which you could feed, but you need to go to the source of your hope. Don't change your spiritual diet during a crisis. Hold onto the Word of God by speaking and meditating on it, day and night. Maintain your spiritual strength by feeding on the Word.

PSALM 119:50
50 This is my comfort in my affliction, for Your word has given me life.

No matter what the affliction is, whether it is your health, finances, emotional issues, or whatever the case may be, you have a direct connection with the Word of God that gives life. Don't change your diet during a crisis because you need the Word of God more than ever. The Lord is your portion, and the Word of God is provided as your delight to give you life and peace.

Chapter Fourteen

YOUR STORY DOES NOT END HERE

YOU MAY BE GOING through a tough time. Circumstances may have dealt you some painful blows. Perhaps you are wondering, *What is coming next? Why is God allowing all these things to happen to me?*

If you feel like there is no hope or things cannot get better, I want to encourage you. This is NOT the end of your story! There is another chapter, a continuation.

ECCLESIASTES 9:4
4 But for him who is joined to all the living there is hope, for a living dog is better than a dead lion.

No matter how bad things are, there is hope. God wants you to know that there is a continuation, and the story has not ended. The Bible says that a living dog is better than a dead lion, which means that it doesn't matter how bad things are. If you are alive, there is hope that something is going to change. The enemy wants you to give up and cave in. But if you cave in, you will not experience what God has in the next chapter of your life.

Don't allow fear or discouragement. Instead, take courage. The Bible says that to him that is joined to all the living, there is hope. The circumstance is not enough to steal your hope because hope is a function of your focus and trust. It is not a result of how good or bad things are. Therefore, you don't have to give up your hope. Instead, you can keep your eyes on God, who is the source of your hope.

PSALM 27:13
13 I would have lost heart, unless I had believed that I would see the goodness of the Lord in the land of the living.

You cannot choose what you experience, but you can choose what you believe. No matter what life throws at you, you don't have to let go of what you believe. The Bible says Abraham, against hope, believed in hope.

ROMANS 4:16-22
16 Therefore it is of faith that it might be according to grace, so that the promise might be sure to all the seed, not only to those who are of the law, but also to those who are of the faith of Abraham, who is the father of us all

17 (as it is written, "I have made you a father of many nations") in the presence of Him whom he believed—God, who gives life to the dead and calls those things which do not exist as though they did;

18 who, contrary to hope, in hope believed, so that he became the father of many nations, according to what was spoken, "So shall your descendants be."

19 And not being weak in faith, he did not consider his own

body, already dead (since he was about a hundred years old), and the deadness of Sarah's womb.

20 He did not waver at the promise of God through unbelief, but was strengthened in faith, giving glory to God,

21 and being fully convinced that what He had promised He was also able to perform.

22 And therefore "it was accounted to him for righteousness."

What is standing contrary to your hope? What has God spoken to you? You can still believe in hope, despite the adversity because you believe in your heart. Your hope will help you change to become what God has said about you. Trials will pass, but the Word of the Lord endures forever.

Nothing can steal your hope without your permission. Your circumstance should not be the barometer for your hope because Christ in you is the hope of glory.

COLOSSIANS 1:27
27 To them God willed to make known what are the riches of the glory of this mystery among the Gentiles: which is Christ in you, the hope of glory.

Christ in you is the guarantee that this situation will not take you out! *Christ in you* is the guarantee that you will not be stuck here forever.

Christ in you is the guarantee that the situation will get better. *Christ in you* is the guarantee that resurrection power is at work on your behalf.

The Living Hope is in you. Your story has not ended. There is a continuation, and it is brighter.

Chapter Fifteen

MISCALCULATION OF ADVERSITY

THERE IS SOMETHING about adversity that makes your faith unshakable and gives you courage! It causes you to be rooted. The enemy thought he could mess with you, your kids, and your family. He thought he could attack your health and your mind. Instead, you drew closer to God and allowed the Word of God to be the lamp unto your feet and the light unto your path.

1 CORINTHIANS 2:6-11

6 However, we speak wisdom among those who are mature, yet not the wisdom of this age, nor of the rulers of this age, who are coming to nothing.

7 But we speak the wisdom of God in a mystery, the hidden wisdom which God ordained before the ages for our glory,

8 which none of the rulers of this age knew; for had they known, they would not have crucified the Lord of glory.

9 But as it is written: "Eye has not seen, nor ear heard, Nor have entered into the heart of man The things which God has prepared for those who love Him."

10 But God has revealed them to us through His Spirit. For the Spirit searches all things, yes, the deep things of God.

11 For what man knows the things of a man except the spirit

of the man which is in him? Even so no one knows the things of God except the Spirit of God.

The "rulers" of whom Paul speaks in verse six are demonic forces ruled by the devil. Paul also said he was speaking the wisdom of God in a mystery—a hidden wisdom. God ordained this wisdom for our glory, but He presented it in such a way that it bypassed the wisdom of this world and the rulers of this age.

They did not know why Jesus was dying. If the rulers of this age had known, they would not have crucified the Lord of Glory. Their crucifying Jesus was a miscalculation, and the Bible reveals it was a setup. The enemy's attack on Jesus was a setup by God, but the enemy did not realize it.

The attack of the enemy on Jesus led to something that happened on the other side. What happened? Through the crucifixion of Jesus, we now have life. By Jesus' death, God opened the way to give life to many other people by having Christ live in them. Because Jesus died and was raised from the dead, He can now be Savior to whoever will call upon His name.

It was a miscalculation by the enemy because they would not have crucified the Lord of glory if they had known that this was God's wisdom being employed. They would have allowed Him to die a natural death.

Because they crucified Jesus, a Man Who knew no sin, He then became sin for us. Through that sacrifice, we can become the righteousness of God. There was a divine exchange. Jesus knew no sin. He was righteous, but He became sin for us. We were sinners, but we became righteous through Him.

There was a miscalculation of adversity. For example, when Moses died, the Spirit of the Lord then rested on Joshua. Moses was taken out of the picture, and God began to speak to Joshua and prepare him. Job is another example. He had much adversity, but many blessings came on him.

DEUTERONOMY 28:7
7 The LORD will cause your enemies who rise against you to be defeated before your face; they shall come out against you one way and flee before you seven ways.

When a thief is found, he must restore sevenfold (Proverbs 6:31 NKJV). The enemy will come against you one way, but he will flee from before you seven ways. That doesn't mean that the enemy merely runs away. Adversity will not leave you the same way it met you. You are going to be in a better place than you were when adversity found you!

Look at that principle. It has often been said, "Let sleeping dogs lie." Why? If you aggravate a sleeping dog, he may bite you. Even if you only poked it a little bit, he would not return in the same way. The dog's response will be sevenfold. He will attack you with great fervor.

God is never going to waste adversity. Your life won't

have to carry labels saying "pre-adversity" and "post-adversity." Your post-adversity existence will be so much different! There is going to be a transformation. If the enemy had known what would happen to your life, he would have left you the way you were. He would have let sleeping dogs lie.

Adversity causes you to build your resolve. You must develop a greater force to stand. If nothing is pushing you, you will not need much strength to stand. If something is coming against you, you will need resistance, fortitude, and determination to stand. That which the enemy meant for evil, God can turn it for your good (Genesis 50:20).

You also come out with a new sense of focus. There is something about adversity that makes you rearrange your life and reprioritize things. You see what is essential. For instance, one of the results that came because of COVID is a sense of focus because people realized that some things that they thought were crucial are not crucial at all. Some of the things they thought were optional are essential.

What are some essentials? The Word of God. Prayer. Praise. Fellowshipping with God. During quarantine, our homes became the church of God. We already knew that our body was a temple, but we realized our home could be a place of worship too. We discovered that we don't need to get to a church building to have a great time with God. But remember that the Word of God also says we should not forsake the assembling of ourselves together.

Chapter Sixteen

FOCUS COMES
OUT OF ADVERSITY

YOU SET YOUR FACE like a flint, and you are trusting God. You wait upon Him for direction. The enemy tries to bring adversity, but you are holding onto the Word of God and speaking it. You are declaring the Word of God.

There are things about the Word you may not have paid attention to before. Now, you are looking for different ways God can speak to you. Your ears are open to the Word of God. You are praying in the Spirit, and your heart is open to receive from Him. You are closer to God.

Psalm 119:71 says: *"It is good for me that I have been afflicted, that I may learn Your statutes."* There is something about adversity that brings you closer to God's Word. By the time you are done, you are not where you were. You are on a different plane, and even the enemy cannot relate to you the same way. Your friends cannot relate to you the same way. You come out with a new sense of focus. You mean business!

What else happens? You have a sense of recovery.

PSALM 30:5
5 For His anger is but for a moment, His favor is for life; Weeping may endure for a night, but joy comes in the morning.

It is not just because you understand things. God brings healing. God brings victory. God brings a word of deliverance. God pulls you out of that dark place and sets your feet upon a rock (Psalm 40:1). Recovery out of adversity happens. You are no longer at the same place. The enemy flees seven ways. There is a recovery of all the enemy tried to steal.

PSALM 66:12
12 You have caused men to ride over our heads; We went through fire and through water; But You brought us out to rich fulfillment.

God will not bring you out into an average place. Instead, he will bring you to rich fulfillment. God can turn things around, and you can go from lack to plenty in an instant! With God, nothing shall be impossible. Nothing!

You come out with a sense of purpose. There is a redefining of things that are important to you, a renewed sense of determination. Focus is moved away from certain things that are not as important. Some people suffer adversity, and afterward, their life's mission is to eradicate that thing from the lives of others. Their sense of purpose was born as they went through adversity.

Your own sense of purpose will be refined and invigorated. You will be more determined that your life will have fresh meaning. There must be purpose after adversity.

God is going to help you bring reason and purpose even through adversity. Second Corinthians 1:4 (NKJV) says, *"Who comforts us in all our tribulation, that we may be able to comfort those who are in any trouble, with the comfort with which we ourselves are comforted by God."* Use the same comfort to help other people. When you go through a situation, you are uniquely equipped to help somebody else. You would not have been able to encourage that person if you hadn't gone through it yourself.

Adversity gives you a sense of purpose. For example, someone may have lost a family member due to a drug overdose. They make it their life's mission to help others who have lost loved ones. Suppose a parent loses a child because of a drunk driver. In that case, that parent will be able to comfort others in the same circumstances. Adversity causes something to rise within us that says, "This is not right, and I am going to use my life to eradicate this thing." Often, great purpose is born out of great pain.

Don't waste your pain in tears alone. Let purpose come out of your pain. What purpose is God trying to bring out of your pain today? What determination will come out of your adversity? What is the comfort you are receiving? That can be the seed for somebody else's comfort.

God wants to bring meaning out of adversity. He wants you to comfort somebody else. There is someone you are destined to impact. People are waiting for you to go through your comforting process so you can bring them through theirs. Some of the music and songs that we enjoy today were born out of great adversity. The Psalms were not written out of context; they were composed because of what David was going through. The comfort David received has been passed on to us, and we can use his psalms to comfort ourselves. You can write your own psalm for someone else to sing. Purpose comes out of adversity.

Look at the way a slingshot is constructed. If we see the pulling of it as the enemy trying to restrain you, we see that tension is created. It causes friction. It feels like you are going backward. Once that adversity leaves, the slingshot snaps back into place. It is propelled forward, and its trajectory changes completely.

The enemy may have attacked, causing devastation, destruction, and ruin, but God is able to engage your recovery so you can do kingdom exploits. We are not just trying to stay in the same place and recover what the enemy has stolen. No! We want to do exploits and go far beyond where we were before.

Chapter Seventeen

YOU SHALL NOT GO OUT EMPTY

YOU ARE NOT COMING out the same! When the Israelites went through 400 years of slavery, they did not come out with "post-adversity" certificates. They came out with spoils. You are not coming out with just a T-shirt. Instead, you are coming out with great spoils. The Bible says, *"You shall not go empty-handed."* (Exodus 3:21).

You will come out with increase. When the Israelites went into Egypt and were under slavery, they did not come out empty. God told them to go and borrow gold and other good things from the Egyptians. They left loaded with good things. God did not allow them to suffer slavery and just come out with nothing. Yes, they were no longer slaves, but that was not enough for God. He wants you to come out with much more than you had when you went in.

Increase! God will crown your year with goodness.

Psalm 65:11 says, *"You crown the year with Your goodness, and Your paths drip with abundance."* God is into restoration, not just recovery. The Lord is interested in multiplication. Recognize that God has certain things on the other side of your adversity that He wants you to experience. He wants you to experience courage, determination, focus, recovery, purpose, and increase.

What is within the hidden wisdom of God during a season of adversity? If the princes of this world had known, they would not have caused you to be laid off unfairly. Family problems and financial problems cause people to turn to God and get wisdom from Him. Wisdom brings us out to a much bigger place.

Is your back against the wall? You can receive wisdom from God that will change your life. It would not have happened without adversity. God has a purpose for your life that cannot be derailed by adversity. It can only be enhanced by whatever adversity the enemy brings your way.

ISAIAH 54:17
17 No weapon formed against you shall prosper, And every tongue which rises against you in judgment You shall condemn. This is the heritage of the servants of the LORD, And their righteousness is from Me," Says the LORD."

Weapons may be fashioned, but they will not prosper. That means even if the enemy expects a weapon to prosper against you, it won't. God is going to turn it for your good. Whatever the setback is, that setback becomes a backdrop for your comeback. Whatever the enemy meant for evil, God is turning it for your good. God will cause that adversity to develop courage and determination in you. It will develop focus, recovery, purpose, and increase in you.

Let the Holy Spirit do a transforming work in your life so that adversity will not cause you to be sidetracked. You can transition to the other side of adversity, to that place where patience is built up so you can be perfect and entire, lacking nothing.

You can come out with courage, determination, focus, recovery, purpose, and increase. May the enemy flee from before you seven ways! May you receive a sevenfold blessing for every trouble!

For your trouble, may you receive double. That shows again that God doesn't intend for you to come out the same way you went in.

ISAIAH 61:7
7 Instead of your shame you shall have double honor, And instead of confusion they shall rejoice in their portion. Therefore, in their land they shall possess double; Everlasting joy shall be theirs.

God is not just interested in removing your shame. He is turning your shame to double honor—Not a double problem, but a double honor! Instead of confusion, you shall rejoice in your portion. Everlasting joy shall be yours!

The Holy Spirit is changing your outlook to an "instead." Instead of shame, double honor. Instead of confusion, joy. This is much more than having shame removed. You move from shame to honor and from honor to double honor!

The Holy Spirit can accelerate processes in your life. Don't assume that because the enemy pushed you backward with adversity, you are just going to be restored to where you were before. Expect a double increase! Expect to be propelled forward.

Whatever the enemy did to bring confusion, hurt, discouragement, tears, hopelessness, worry, and fear, God will bring rejoicing. You will rejoice in your portion. Whatever may have caused confusion was a miscalculation of adversity. God is turning it around. Instead of having confusion, you will rejoice!

Therefore, in your land (not in heaven), you shall possess double and everlasting joy shall be yours. Thank God for His Word!

Your story is not ended. In the end, there is rejoicing! Until there is rejoicing, your story is not over.

A PRAYER OF SALVATION

Father, thank You for sending Your Son, Jesus Christ, to die for me on the cross. I believe in my heart that Jesus is the Son of God, that He died on the cross, and that He rose again from the dead. I confess that He is my Lord and Savior. I commit my life to You; come into my life and be my Lord and Savior.

In Jesus' name,

Amen

ABOUT THE AUTHOR

'Lanre Somorin MD is a triple board-certified psychiatrist and has been practicing since 1995. He is also an associate pastor. He has a specialty in Addiction Psychiatry.

Somorin's mission is to help people discover hope and to live purposeful lives. Somorin is the medical director for an outpatient mental health facility with seven clinical sites.

He has been listed in the Top Doctors' issue of the Hudson Valley (NY) Magazine yearly since 2006. He owned and operated an outpatient substance abuse rehab facility and has held various leadership positions, including clinical consultant to the Army Substance Abuse Clinic in West Point, NY. He has a private behavioral health practice in Monroe, NY. He is married and is the father of two.

ALSO BY THE AUTHOR

SEIZE YOUR MOMENT

In *Seize Your Moment, Unmasking Everyday Opportunities*, board-certified psychiatrist and associate pastor 'Lanre Somorin, MD, reveals thirty-one keys to overcoming the barriers that prevent us from capitalizing on what daily life has to offer. Combining scripture with practical tools, motivational quotes, and insightful advice, Somorin empowers readers to take full control of their lives.

Starting with the vital role preparation plays in identifying and taking advantage of opportunities, Somorin explores the need for understanding and wisdom, tips for dealing with adversity, and the importance of removing distractions. You'll discover how the simplest ideas often represent opportunity and recognize that successfully capitalizing on opportunity does not mean avoiding hard work.

seizeyourmomentnow.com

ALSO BY THE AUTHOR

THE POWER OF A NEW BEGINNING

Roadblocks and set backs don't have the final say in your life! There is power in a new beginning to transition you into an area that is greater in scope, greater in fulfillment, and greater in resources. The ability to transition into this new beginning is available to you.

Associate Pastor and Board Certified Psychiatrist, 'Lanre Somorin, M.D., reveals important truths about the adversities that stand in the way of transition into greater, identifying these hindrances and explaining how to overcome them.

The Power of a New Beginning is a book designed to enable you to firmly grasp your destiny and transition into the greater that God has established for you. Step into your new beginning today!

ALSO BY THE AUTHOR

TRANSITION TO GREATER

God is able to do much more than we can think or imagine. However, there is a limit to what God can do in our lives based on what we are doing right now. We often say we are waiting on God, but God requires us to position ourselves if we are going to experience greater.

In his compelling book, *Transition to Greater*, 'Lanre Somorin M.D. challenges us to remove the limitations that have been keeping us from experiencing the abundant life God has designed for us.

FOR MORE
INFORMATION

Contact:

www. lanresomorin.com

Bibliography

1   "Benjamin Franklin Quotes." BrainyQuote.com. Brainy-
Media Inc, 2021. 28 May 2021. https://www.brainyquote.com/
quotes/benjamin_franklin_138217

2   "William Arthur Ward." AZQuotes.com. Wind and Fly
LTD, 2021. 28 May 2021. https://www.azquotes.com/quote/564420

3   Mason, John. Fall Seven Times Stand up Eight: How to
Succeed No Matter What, by John Mason, Christian Art Publish-
ers, 2016.